LifeOPedia

By Annanya Desai

Made with ❤️ on the Notion Press Platform

www.notionpress.com

Content

Content

Preface

This book is a compilation of blogs I wrote and published between the ages of 12 and 13. During the lockdown, writing became my way of making sense of the world and expressing myself. What started as a simple hobby quickly turned into a passion, and through these blogs, I found the power of words and the joy of sharing my thoughts with others.

Each entry in this book reflects a moment in time, capturing my thoughts, observations, and experiences as I navigated through the world as a young teenager. From personal reflections to exploring new perspectives, these blogs are a journey of growth, learning, and self-discovery.

Writing these blogs helped me navigate through uncertain times and discover new aspects of myself. I hope that as you read through these pages, you find something that speaks to you, makes you smile, or inspires you in some way. Thank you for joining me on this journey. I hope you enjoy reading these blogs as much as I enjoyed writing them.

I Caught A Smile

It was a dismal morning. I had forgotten to set my alarm. I thought I was late for online school. I got ready in a few minutes, gobbled my breakfast, only to realise that it was a holiday. My stomach began to ache because I had eaten so quickly. I sat and sulked and felt miserable. Then I suddenly remembered that I had an online open house at school. Well, ofcourse, I missed my slot, and there I was, waiting for forty-two children to finish their turn, before I could go. Just Great!

I decided to make a fresh glass of lemonade to brighten my day. I heard the doorbell ring. I opened the door. It was the washerman. He smiled and asked for his pay. I nodded bleakly and gave him the money kept aside for him. He took the money and sent a big grin my way. This time, something happened to me. I smiled back. Suddenly, the day didn't seem so bad. I caught myself smiling multiple times that day. I smiled while doing my homework, while exercising and evening washing my hands. I flashed a smile towards everyone I saw and they all smiled back.

It felt as though I was the one making everyone happy, and crazy as it sounds, I was!

Smiling is contagious! When you smile, the world smiles back.

Scientists and spiritual teachers alike agree that the simple act of smiling can transform you and lift the mood of everyone around you. Smiling makes you happy. It makes you appear more attractive to others and it can even lengthen your life. So, before you continue reading, slap on a nice genuine smile on your face.

When you smile, something magical happens inside your brain. It's like a little party that makes you feel happy and healthy. Smiling helps your brain release special chemicals that can make stress go away. These chemicals, called neuropeptides, work like tiny helpers to fight off bad feelings.

But that's not all! Smiling also brings out other happy chemicals like dopamine, serotonin, and endorphins. Dopamine and serotonin make you feel good and cheerful. Endorphins are like your body's own little superheroes, making pain go away and making you feel better.

There are so many good things about smiling! It can help you feel less stressed, lower your blood pressure, make your immune system stronger, give you more energy, and even make pain hurt less. Smiling is like a superpower that makes you feel great!

In the end, smiling is a simple way to bring lots of good things into your life. It's a magical trick that helps you feel happy, healthy, and strong. A small smile can make a big difference!

So Smile! Grin from ear to ear! Make yourself and the people around you more lively and happy! Send a Smile and watch it weave its magic!

Dance In The Rain

Dark clouds cover the sky, not a ray of light to be seen, gloomy does the day become, but only for those who are unaware of the wonders to come.

Most people find the rain gloomy, it makes them feel lazy, grumpy, stressed and sometimes sad. But it can teach you a lot in life.

"Life isn't about waiting for the storm to pass. It's learning to dance in the rain" - **Vivian Greene**

The best thing that one can do when it's raining, is to let it rain and make the most out of it. So, dance in the rain, smell the fresh fragrance of the earth, see the green grass and the swaying field of growing corn.

A little rain falls into everyone's life. Things don't always work out the way you want them to. But, remember there is an opportunity lurking behind every negative situation. Seize it and forge ahead. Sometimes the storm will just come to clear your path and loosen your soil, so you can GROW in all different directions.

The Path To A Better You

Self-Improvement is the key to creating the better life that people desire.

Everyone wants to achieve prosperity, have more love in their life, and achieve greater success and happiness, and we all know this is not easy.

We humans are naturally born competitive. Winning causes us to have an adrenaline rush and also gives us a reason to be proud of ourselves.

Self-Improvement means competing with yourself. It infact implies that we should all strive to do a particular thing better than we did it last time.

One of the biggest importance of self-improvement is the positive impact it has on mental health. When you work on yourself, you get to know yourself better, which lets you deal with your thoughts and emotions more effectively. I would say; Don't learn only from success stories but also from failure stories. Learn about how they fell and don't repeat the same mistakes. Chase your vision and dream passionately and success will start following you.

The hard work of fighting for what's right includes the hard work of mastering yourself and taking good care of yourself. It's not selfish to spend time improving yourself. In order to be there for each other, we have to first be there for ourselves.

The Magic Of A Friendship

Friendship is one of the most important and valuable things in our life. To live without friendship is life without living. Human interaction is necessary for survival, but developed friendships are the key to anyone's well-being. A famous philosopher Euripides once said, "Friends show their love in times of trouble, not in happiness".

A true friend makes you feel special, shares your joys and sorrows. He is not envious of your achievements and accomplishments, instead he watches your success with great delight. He cannot make your problems disappear, but he gives you good advice and a shoulder to cry on. He will always tell you the truth, keep all your secrets. A true friend is able to see the pain in your eyes while others see the smile on your face. He makes you smile when you have forgotten how to. He lifts you up when you cannot lift yourself.

True friendship is precious and rare. You are blessed if you have found one or two or three such friends in your life. Friendship is being foolish together. Friendship is being mad together. It is being everything together.

True friends are like family, precious inspite of their shortcomings and frailties. They may even hurt us at times but in the end they have our wellbeing at heart and cannot be replaced.

"A single rose can be my garden, a single friend can be my world" - **Leo Buscaglia**

From Failure To Fortune

Remember how we learned to walk and cycle? We failed several times before learning how to do so. But the sad truth is that we were taught that winning deserves praise and failure ridicule.

Are you aware that Amitabh Bachchan had once tried to get a job in "All India Radio" ? He was rejected. They found his voice unsuitable; Michael Jordan was cut from the school's basketball team; Steeve Jobs was fired from his own Company; Abraham Lincoln lost eight elections. This makes me realise that the greatest achievers have had far more 'failures' than they have 'successes"

Failure is definitely not the end of the road. Rather, it is a great teacher. It shows us how to tread the right path. Failure makes us think. We realise what people go through when they fail and how they cope, to succeed later. It makes you realise what you have done wrong, so you can do the right, later. If you have never failed, it means that you have never tried something new.

The fear of failure is the greatest barrier to success. It is also the major reason that holds back people from realizing their full potential and achieving their goal.

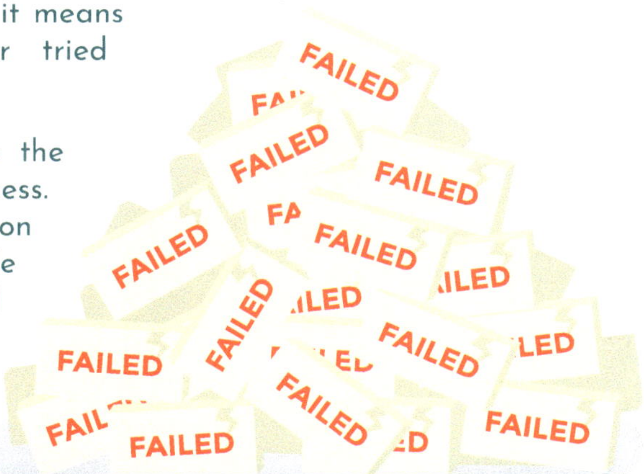

Playing it safe can also be risky. It puts you out of action. You choose to let go of the potential opportunities and push yourself into mediocrity. When you restrict yourself to your cocoon, you keep yourself from tapping your full potential and blooming into a beautiful butterfly.

Failure is a matter of perspective. Many think of failure as the opposite of success. But failures are infact, the stepping stones to success. Nothing worthwhile in life has ever been achieved without a series of failures.

Thomas Alva Edison once said:- "I did not fail 1,000 times, but I found out 1,000 ways that didn't work".

Turning Wounds Into Wisdom

Turn Your Wounds Into Wisdom - **Oprah Winfrey**.

This quote has most certainly changed the way I looked at failure, success and life as a whole. It conveys that some of life's best lessons are learnt while we are going through hard times.

The greatest setbacks in our life often end up being great blessings in disguise, but only if we accept them as such. If we have courage to learn from our failures and try once again, we can achieve great success. So, when you have a choice of either getting up and moving forward after you fail or just laying there, showing signs of weakness don't think about it, get up and keep moving. It doesn't matter how many times you have fallen, get up once again and learn from your mistakes, so you don't make them again.

Wayne Dyer once said, "When you change the way you look at things, the way things look change".

Always have a positive mindset. Don't look at obstacles as problems. Look at them as challenges. All challenges are made for you to overcome, you just have to believe that you can and you will.

Now give it some thought and remember, we must move on from our deepest wounds, but not forget them.

Believing is Achieving

Believe you can and you're half way there - Theodore Roosevelt.

When you believe you can, you will. Even when times seem hard, never stop believing that you can and never stop believing in yourself. When you keep trying to find success and keep believing that you will, you will receive it. When you want to achieve something in life, the first thing you must do is to believe that you can achieve that something.

Your dreams and goals will be pointless, if you do not believe that you can achieve them, because you'll be second guessing your capability and doubting your skills to actually take the necessary actions. But when you believe you can, quitting and giving up do not belong to your vocabulary.

People who succeed are those who have the courage and determination to take the first step towards their goals. They don't need much to start doing it, they just believe that they can, and guess what? they are halfway there!

Strength In Unity

Unity it starts with YOU, ends with WE and brings Success.

If we all remain united, we will not be defeated. Even when everyone on planet Earth is going through difficult times, it makes the situation much better when we realise that we are all going through it together, and understand that everyone is there for you.

We all know the story of the farmer and his quarrelling sons. The sons could each easily break a single stick, but when several sticks were made into a bundle, none of them could break it. The sons then realized the value of UNITY and gave up their quarrels.

We understand from this that peace and success come from overcoming our differences. If we are not united, we will all fall, only to learn our lesson and get back together.

Unity is strength and if we all, inspite of our differences in race, gender, ethnicity, etc. come together and work towards a common purpose, we are more likely to succeed.

An Alternative Perspective

A perspective is a way one looks at and thinks about something. Everyone has a different understanding of a situation, it can either be positive or negative, it's just the way you look at it. Whether you want it to be a 9 or a 6 is completely up to you. It is also important that you seek to understand another's perspective. When you judge someone wrong, it is because you don't understand how their reasoning works. But what if May be they are right?

So, instead of looking for an outcome that is negative or has some flaw, look for something beneficial or something that adds to your life. By shifting your search for happiness, you can create it.

Wayne Dyer once said, "If you change the way you look at things, the things you look at change". Very true. A few hundred years ago, Galileo Galilei proved that the sun did not orbit the earth and that in fact, it is the earth which moves around the sun. Until then, humans believed that the giant ball of light orbited the earth. This changed everything about our reality until that point of time. When Galileo Galilei observed the night sky with his telescope, he saw completely different. By thinking differently.

Be Yourself

Be yourself, everyone else is already taken - **Oscar Wilde**

You may have been told or heard that you should always be yourself ? But what does it mean. Being yourself means you like and know who you are. Being yourself means having self-respect. And it means living life the way you want to live it, not based on others' thoughts. Don't get worked up on other people's opinions, you can't control them or their thoughts.

"Your time is limited, so don't waste it living someone else's life" - **Steve Jobs**

There is only one of you in this world. No two others are the same. You are rare and imperfectly perfect. Sometimes we tend to compare ourselves to others, and worry about what the world thinks of us and suffer because of that. Don't be trapped by dogma - which is living with the results of another's thinking - and you will understand who you truly are, what you truly want to do and will finally understand the power of your inner voice.

Happiness and success will come to YOU because YOU decided to BE YOURSELF!

Imagination Creates Reality

The true sign of intelligence is not knowledge but imagination - **Albert Einstein**

Knowledge is the information, understanding and skills you have gained and stored in your brain. Imagination is the ability to create things – real or not – from the information in your brain.

Knowledge is necessary but it is imagination that gives it wings to soar. For knowledge is limited, whereas imagination embraces the entire universe, giving birth to unlimited possibilities.

The greatest innovators of all times had the ability to deal with real-life situations by using the power of the creative mind. Imagination allows one to solve problems in ways that have not yet been used. Innovation can't really exist without imagination and out-of-box thinking. We have discovered and unveiled the greatest mysteries because Sir Isaac Newton, Albert Einstein and many more people were curious and used their imagination and believed it was possible in the end, it was !

Don's stop. There are many more wonders for you to discover. Keep imagining, keep thinking, keep believing and you will keep inventing.

Thinking Differently

We cannot solve our problems with the same thinking we used when we created them - **Albert Einstein**

When we create problems, we do so because we can't see through them or we can't see outside the box (the problem). If we stay where we are, unable to understand the problem, we will never find the solution.

Imagine a glass elevator on the side of a very tall building. The view from each floor is different and the higher you go the bigger and broader the view.

When you see the problems as a whole, every detail included, it'll look a load different than it did when you looked at it with a narrow mind. Break down the make-believe barrier inside your head. Extend your view, change your perspective, step out of the box and solve your problem.

How?

Get rid of all the unhelpful thoughts and prove them wrong, turn the situation upside down and find patterns never spotted before; think differently and believe maybe it's possible? And lastly shift your view and open your mind to every possible answer. The solution is apparent, if you see the same problem from a view that's different.

Be A Rainbow In Their Cloud

We all go through tough times and we all have bad moments. Most people tend to focus on what they have gone through instead of the people who have helped them through the hard times. The people who become the shining bright stars in their dull grey sky, the silver lining in their dark cloud, and the colorful rainbow in it. The people who cared and gave them enthusiastic support, when they required it the most. Don't you remember the people who made your life just a little better when you felt miserable.

Now it's time to give back!

Think about all those people and how amazing they are and how their one small deed possibly made you feel safe and okay. Be one of those people for another person. Show your kindness and love to them, make them happy and believe me you will be too.

Worries

Worrying - It's imagining something you don't want to happen. Instead of solving tomorrow's problems, it takes away today's peace and it gives small things a big halo!

Worrying – It stops you from thinking big, achieving big and being big.

You often find yourself in places you didn't wish to be and when you are there, fear strikes you, a fear that tells you that things are going to get worse and then you start worrying about that, what lies ahead. But why worry?

Why worry when you know that what lies ahead is meant to be. Why worry when after making a mistake comes a big chance, a chance to change. Why worry when after every stinging pain comes peace and then joy. Why worry when you believe that the most confusing problems can be resolved. Worrying too much never gets you anywhere, working hard to eliminate your worries does.

Beauty lies within little things

Enjoy the little things in life, for one day you'll look back and realise they were big things.

Do you remember smiling at the memory of something small, maybe just a moment with you family? Those little periods of time are where the beauty of life lies.

Notice the little things around. Notice the small things that give you happiness, gaze at the daffodils or the little children playing in the park. If something makes your soul smile, it will always make your soul smile, even through the toughest moments. Life is made up of many small happy memories. And if you can collect these memories, you will always feel satisfied.

When everything seems confusing or incomplete, the happy memories will remind you that happiness still exists, and bit by bit everything will complete itself.

Enjoy The Small Things, They Are Everything.

Remember the poem "Daffodils" by William Wordsworth? These small things will flash upon your inward eye when you are lonely or sad and fill your heart with pleasure.

Don't Mind Criticism

Don't Mind Criticism! If it is untrue, disregard it; If it is unfair, don't let it irritate you; If it is justified, learn from it.

We receive a lot of criticism that is, in simple terms false. Ignore it. Do not give people the attention that they don't deserve.

Many times, you receive unfair criticism which is patently wrong and you feel your blood rise and heart pound. In this case, keep calm! Repeat your point but open your mind to see from both perspectives. Only then you will know what's right.

There is also something known as constructive criticism, where people point out your mistakes or give suggestions politely only for you to learn from them. Value such criticism.

Embracing Opportunities

If Opportunity doesn't knock, build a door - **Milton Berle**

Sometimes, its all about taking the right initiatives, instead of waiting for opportunity to come. Relying on chance to get you somewhere isn't really going to work. It's up to you to stand up and say, "I am going to accomplish my goals".

It's up to you to stand up and build a door, a door, you know, opportunity is compelled to knock on. And then when opportunity knocks, you open the door with a joyful face. "Carpe Diem" or "Seize the Day"! Opportunity doesn't knock twice.

So go and build your door, go and figure out what success feels like. Take the initiative to increase the chances of you growing. Go, and build a door!

The Secret To Productivity

Wake up with determination, Go to bed with satisfaction

Easy right? No, there is much more to productivity than you think. It is not just what you do with time but how you run your mind during that particular amount of time. It is rightly said by Paul J. Meyer – "Productivity is never an accident. It is always a result of a commitment to excellence, intelligent planning and focused effort".

Being productive means setting goals for yourself, higher every time. When you achieve your goals, your self-esteem rockets. You keep challenging yourself. Striving to overcome obstacles, gives you energy, focus and conviction. You'll do more with the time you have. There certainly aren't enough hours in a day to do all the things we wish to do. Being productive gives us a chance to find time, the time we thought never existed. This allows us to do more in lesser time.

If the 'more" that you have begun doing is important, if it makes you feel free and warm, if it makes you happy, then it's worth spending your time on. Writing makes me happy. I consider this to be a productive use of my time.

Here are some tips to be more productive :-

- Keeping To-Do Lists will keep you moving forward, and committing to them helps you finish doing the important things.
- Check-Lists really help to track progress and your journey to productivity.
- Reminders and Calendars keep you on schedule

And finally :-

"The key is not to prioritize what's on your schedule, but to schedule your priorities" - **Stephan R. Covey**

Shed The Weight

If you want to fly, you have to give up everything that weighs you down - **Toni Morrison**

In life, it is very necessary to remove the burden that's pulling you down, to push away those things that are preventing you from flying high and to cut loose those strings attached to you. Sometimes those things are pretty hard to lose, sometimes there are a lot of emotional attachments with those things. But if those things are drawing you back, it's most beneficial to stay away from them.

When I say "stay away", I mean to let go of all the close or even the people that you are not familiar with, that keep trying to pull you down. First, we need to identify those kinds of people, then, it's time to let go and fly high.

Surround yourself with people who love, understand and respect you. Surround yourself with people who are happy for your achievements. Surround yourself with people that you can learn from.

Perfectly Imperfect

One of the basic rules of this Universe is that NOTHING IS PERFECT.

We all have our flaws, we all have our dents and our scratches, we have our broken smiles and weird personalities. But that's who we are and it's okay. It's okay to be perfectly imperfect.

Nothing in this world is flawless. Perfection simply doesn't exist. Without imperfection, humans would have nothing to learn and nothing to strive for. Perfection is impossible because it means being flawless, it means not being able to make mistakes, not being able to misunderstand, it means not being human.

The term "human" means that you will make blunders, it means you will fail, but it's all to overcome with experience, to learn, to grow. Your mistakes are what have gotten you where you are and your faults are what have made you who you are.

Remember:

"We all have imperfections, and that's perfectly okay!"

Perseverance Prevails

To persist in anything undertaken, maintain a purpose in spite of the difficulty in doing something, despite difficulty or delay in achieving success.

When a child first learns to stand up and tries to walk, he falls down again and again, but by nature and instinct, he gets up and again tries to step forward, although again he falls down. But in the end, he succeeds in walking.

In spite of his repeated failures along the road to success, a person who perseveres finally achieves his goals. A persevering person is one who has tremendous self-confidence, indomitable determination, a natural urge towards hard work and untiring energy to continue trying again, without grumbling or expressing dissatisfaction.

'Perseverance' in my eyes, is something that makes common people stand out. Everything you want to succeed in, boils down to whether you have the quality of perseverance. You may be extremely talented, you may be outstandingly smart, but without the push of perseverance, it really doesn't work. Perseverance gives us the ability to see our dreams become reality.

Once Gone, Forever Gone

Once gone, forever gone,

The time that's misused.

Once gone, forever gone,

The word once it's spoken.

Once gone, forever gone,

The opportunity one wasted.

Once gone, forever gone,

The occasion that's missed.

Once gone, forever gone,

The day that is forgotten.

After the completion of an action, you can't go back. Once it's done, it's done. So before regret has a chance to haunt you, think. Think before every word, every action, because what is done cannot be undone.

The Gratitude Effect

I recently attended an orientation at my sister's college, where they talked about being grateful and its importance. Being grateful for the little things diverts our attention from our problems. It diverts our attention away from the things we lack to abundance that is already present. We smile more when we are grateful, we feel blessed and happy when we are grateful. Once we make this a practice, we remain forever happy.

We tend to forget just how lucky we are; so I advise you to take out a small notebook every day and write down the things you are grateful for. After a few days, you can read about the little things that lit fire in you slowly burning your problems away.

"Gratitude is a powerful catalyst for happiness. It's the spark that lights a fire of joy in your soul" - **Amy Collette**.

Great Things Take Time

It took me a long time to understand the concept of patience. I was brought up being told that patience is a virtue but never understood why. So today we are going to unravel that mystery and understand how powerful patience is.

I was folding a swan out of origami with my sister one day. Being me, I took it as a competition and quickly made a swan in just 2 minutes. Seeing that my sister wasn't done yet, I sat down beside her, watching how she was making her swan. Eventually, I got bored and decided to take a nap. When I woke up, my sister enthusiastically came running towards me with her paper swan in her hand. To be honest, it looked much more majestic than my floppy swan. I went to my mom sobbing and asked her why I couldn't make such a pretty swan. Then she told me something I will never forget. She said, "You have to be patient while working with origami. Great things take time."

I like to think about it this way: we've all heard the common saying, "Rome wasn't built in a day." Rome took approximately 1,010,450 days to build. That's a long time. With patience, we can not only do, but also refine.

The Real Goal Of Practice

Practice doesn't make perfect. Just reading that line makes us uncomfortable, right? I have been brought up being told one line and one line only: "Practice makes perfect." As I was thinking of topics to write about, I started second-guessing this statement, and a quote came to my mind almost immediately: "Perfect practice makes perfect." You see, just practising isn't the full story, practising properly is.

If we practise poorly without correcting our mistakes, we will just get better at making those mistakes. Practice creates habits, not improvements. Practising perfectly, on the other hand, improves our performance in any skill. It corrects our mistakes and, overall, makes us better.

This is one of the most important things that my ballet teacher has ever taught me. Several factors go into dancing perfectly. In ballet, all of them come with perfect practice. Something as simple as pointing your feet can go wrong in many ways if not given proper attention.

Pay attention to what you are doing while practising. Make sure you are working on correcting your mistakes and becoming better.Practice doesn't make perfect, practising perfectly does.

A Life Of Uncertainty

Once, my family and I planned to leave for a long car ride to Lonavala - a wonderful hill-station in India. We planned to reach at One O'clock and eat our lunch in the hotel itself. We opened Google Maps, and it indicated we would reach there by One O'clock if we left at eight. We followed that and left early that day. But, halfway there, our car came to a halt. As my parents tried to fix the problem, I looked out of the window. The hill sloped down slowly. A lake, calm, clear, and serene lay at the bottom of the hill. The sky was powder blue with whitest clouds I have ever seen. Life didn't feel real at that moment. It took an hour and a half to get the car to start again. We missed the buffet lunch at the restaurant, but it didn't matter. The view I saw at that moment and the feeling I had when I breathed in the warm fresh air put a smile on my face that I couldn't get rid of.

I imagined how I would not have had that feeling of warmth and wonder if something unpredictable, like our car developing a snag hadn't occurred.

"If life were predictable, it would cease to be life, and be without flavour" - **Eleanor Roosevelt**.

Imagine you knew everything that would happen in your future. What would you think would happen then?

- You would not have the same feeling of joy you'd get after winning a competition.
- You wouldn't be surprised to see the gifts the people who care for you brought when you least expected them.
- You'd forget the overwhelming feeling while taking a risk because you knew it would turn out OK.
- You'd know everything that is to come, no surprises no suspense. Life would just be a colorless canvas.

Life's uncertainty is the color you use to paint the beautiful painting you named 'Life'. You don't know what tomorrow would bring you, and that's the entire point of life. You want to keep going to see how different tomorrow will be and the surprises you are yet to witness. Remember there is always something good coming, the future will always be a surprise, but to make the surprises better, we must concentrate on the present.

The joy of life lies in its unpredictability.

Couldn't Do Vs Didn't Do

A few days ago, I started writing a new blog post. I knew the topic would have been fascinating to write and read about. I wrote a sentence and then nothing. The slide was as blank as it could be, a plain white rectangle. I could have finished writing it and gone to sleep with confidence, but I got distracted and didn't.

I am sure all of us plan to achieve new goals every year. There are obstacles we have to overcome. The year isn't as long as one might imagine it to be, to make the best out of it. Ask yourself only two questions, 'Should you?' and 'Can you'? If the answer to both is 'Yes', don't procrastinate, you might forget to do it later.

But sometimes there's another more important task to complete, or it's not possible for you to do X at that moment. In those cases, we should change our priorities. It's all right you couldn't achieve what you had set your sights on. Still, if you didn't do what needed to be done, that regret will set your self-esteem and morale back a long way and hold you back from achieving greater successes in the future.

But it's important to not be striving to achieve unrealistic goals that result in negative emotions such as disappointment, frustration and feeling like a failure. Prioritizing your tasks and walk on step by step, remembering that even a small victory is a victory. This will make achieving your goals easier and simpler.

Push through and finish. It can be difficult, but the end result will make it all worthwhile.

The End Or The Beginning?

When reaching a dead end, one tends to waste time stressing and overanalyzing the situation to figure out a solution that might help you in solving the problem. It's frustrating to see yourself unsuccessful time and again. At times like this, you must start again! On a fresh, brand new page, full of brand new opportunities. Go for it again, this time with a new mindset. I promise you, it'll turn out much better.

While practicing ballet, I hit dead ends too, and more often than not, I couldn't perfect the step! At times like these, I think of the very first things I learned when I attended my first ballet class, 8 years ago. I take a break, stretch and when I'm ready, I try the step again but this time with a different approach, and this time I succeed!

Erase your drawing, start again with a fresh new paper, and with this new mindset, you are going to sketch something much better than before. And this sketch, you'll be sure to frame!

Consistency Is Key

Being consistent is something many of us, including me, struggle with. I find it hard to continue with the things I start, unaware of the reasons. I just stop. I tell myself it's out of laziness or loss of interest, that I do not build up my hobbies to their greatest potential. There are many times I find myself wondering "what if I would have continued?"

Being consistent is hard. It's hard to continue because, today, there are so many different things you can do and learn. We find ourselves shifting interests often and lose interest in the things that once sparked a fire in us.

I have now learnt, that to continue, to be consistent is very important. Continuing is like climbing a staircase, each step representing a stage in your journey. With every step you take, you learn something new. But you will never know this feeling unless you take that second step and once you have, I doubt you will stop.

Being Consistent is the key to creating something that you will be proud of. It is the key to progress that will speed your journey to achieve something you desire. Consistency Is The Key!

Acknowledgement

Thirteen-year-old Annanya could only dream that the random thoughts she began to pen down during the lockdown would someday be published. Now, that dream has come true, and it is all thanks to my grandmother, who inspired me to write, my grandfather, who made sure to comment on every single one of my blogs, and last but not least, my parents and my sister, who introduced me to different perspectives of the world.

It is not without the unwavering support of my family and friends that I have the opportunity and confidence to showcase my work to the world. I would like to especially thank my grandmother, Mrs. Kavita Sajeja, for using her expertise to read, edit, and fine-tune the chapters of this book. To my grandfather, Mr. Chaturbhuj Sajeja, your efforts did not go unnoticed. You printed out the chapters, making it easier for Nani to edit, then compiled them back into a document and emailed each and every one of them to me. It is her dedication and your constant excitement about the book's publication that pushed this project forward.

To my family and friends, your encouragement has been my strength. This book is as much yours as it is mine. Thank you for believing in me and making this dream a reality.

Life is like riding a bicycle.
To keep your balance
you must keep moving.

Albert Einstein

www.ingramcontent.com/pod-product-compliance
Lightning Source LLC
LaVergne TN
LVHW021348160826
845679LV00008B/1533

* 9 7 9 8 8 9 6 7 3 5 3 5 9 *